FRENCH COOKING

Food photography by Peter Barry
Edited by Jillian Stewart
Designed by Claire Leighton
Recipes styled by Jacqueline Bellafontaine
Incidental photography: Gamma, Paris
                                  Telegraph Colour Library, London

2708 French Cooking
This edition published in 1997 by CLB
Distributed in the U.S.A. by BHB International, Inc.
30 Edison Drive, Wayne, New Jersey 07470
© 1992 CLB International
All rights reserved
Printed and bound in Singapore
ISBN 1-85833-679-1

FRENCH COOKING

CLB

INTRODUCTION

French cuisine is justly acclaimed as the best in the world. It is imaginative, exciting, inspired and delicious. To the French cooking is an art, something to be treated with respect and with tender loving care. Unfortunately this philosophy leads many to believe French cooking is difficult and beyond their skill as a cook. This is just not so. The most important element in French cooking is the quality and freshness of the ingredients, not the complexity of the dish.

The forefather of today's style of French cooking was François Pierre de La Varenne. It was he who, in the sixteenth century, advocated a move away from the use of strong spices and flavors to the use of meat juices, butter and subtle sauces to enhance a dish. This tradition continued through the centuries, but added to it was the importance attached to the serving and final appearance of the meal. It is this, the care taken to the final appearance of a dish, that has created the rather mystical aura surrounding French cooking. A great amount of care is taken with the final presentation of a meal, but this is something that never comes before the actual taste of a meal. It is the French passion for food that has earned it its place in history, and the humble country stew is as much a part of that story as the most beautiful creation from a Paris restaurant.

Classic French cuisine owes a great debt to good old fashioned country cooking. In the regions of France the varying local produce was used to create dishes that have remained among the best-known and loved of the repertoire, and it is these dishes that remain the backbone of French cuisine. Burgundy, for example, is first and foremost known for its wines and it is a combination of wine and chicken which makes up the region's most renowned dish, *Coq au Vin.*

The orchards of Normandy produce cider apples and many dishes from this area combine apples, cider or *Calvados,* and cream. And both Brittany and Normandy are famous for *Moules Mariniere,* a delicious combination of mussels and cream. Moving south, recipes from warm and colorful regions such as Provence are full of herbs, tomatoes and peppers and it is from here that *Ratatouille* and *Salade Niçoise* originate.

And who could forget Paris and its surrounding areas. It was here that *haute cuisine* was born. The restaurants of Paris are synonymous with good taste and fine dining and it is the areas surrounding the capital that provide many of the top quality ingredients needed. Besides the local vegetable crops, wild mushrooms and strawberries grow abundantly, providing the restaurants with a convenient supply of fresh produce.

Each region of France has contributed to the national cuisine and this great diversity in taste and style is reflected within these pages. From appetizers to classic meat dishes and desserts, *French Cooking* has a dish to suit every taste and every occasion.

The beautiful and impressive medieval cathedral of Chartres.

Moules Marinière

Preparation Time: 30 minutes **Cooking Time:** 15 minutes **Serves:** 4

Brittany and Normandy are famous for mussels and for cream and so cooks combined the two in one perfect seafood dish.

Ingredients

3lbs mussels
1½ cups dry cider or white wine
4 shallots, finely chopped
1 clove garlic, crushed

1 bouquet garni
½ cup heavy cream
3 tbsps butter, cut into small pieces
2 tbsps finely chopped parsley

Scrub the mussels well and remove the beards and any barnacles from the shells. Discard any mussels that have cracked shells and do not open when lightly tapped. Put the mussels into a large bowl and soak in cold water for at least 1 hour. Meanwhile, chop the parsley very finely.

Bring the cider or wine to the boil in a large stock pot and add the shallots, garlic and bouquet garni. Add the mussels, cover the pan and cook for 5 minutes. Shake the pan or stir the mussels around frequently until the shells open. Lift out the mussels into a large soup tureen or individual serving bowls. Discard any mussels that have not opened. Reduce the cooking liquid by about half and strain into another saucepan. Add the cream and bring to the boil to thicken slightly. Beat in the butter, a few pieces at a time. Adjust the seasoning, add the parsley and pour the sauce over the mussels to serve.

The world-famous Gothic church of Notre-Dame, silhouetted against the sunset.

Artichauts Aioli

Preparation Time: 30 minutes **Cooking Time:** 25 minutes **Serves:** 4

Home-made mayonnaise is in a class by itself. With the addition of garlic, it makes a perfect sauce for artichokes – a typically Provençal appetizer.

Ingredients
4 medium-sized globe artichokes
1 slice lemon
1 bay leaf
Pinch salt

Sauce Aioli
2 egg yolks
1 cup olive oil
2 cloves garlic, peeled and crushed
Salt, pepper and lemon juice to taste
Chervil leaves to garnish

To prepare the artichokes, break off the stems and twist to remove any tough fibres. Trim the base so that the artichokes will stand upright. Trim the points from all the leaves and wash the artichokes well. Bring a large saucepan or stock pot full of water to the boil with the slice of lemon and bay leaf. Add a pinch of salt and, when the water is boiling, add the artichokes. Allow to cook for 25 minutes over moderate heat. While the artichokes are cooking, prepare the sauce.

Whisk the egg yolks and garlic with a pinch of salt and pepper in a deep bowl or in a liquidizer or food processor. Add the olive oil a few drops at a time while whisking by hand, or in a thin, steady stream with the machine running. If preparing the sauce by hand, once half the oil is added, the remainder may be added in a thin, steady stream. Add lemon juice once the sauce becomes very thick. When all the oil has been added, adjust the seasoning and add more lemon juice to taste.

When the artichokes are cooked, the bottom leaves will pull away easily. Remove them from the water with a draining spoon and drain upside-down on paper towels or in a colander. Allow to cool and serve with the sauce aioli. Garnish with chervil.

The impressive facade of the Conciergerie in Paris reflected in the River Seine.

Pâté de Campagne

Preparation Time: 25 minutes **Cooking Time:** 2 hours **Serves:** 10

This is the pâté of French restaurants known also as pâté maison or terrine de chef. It should be coarse textured.

Ingredients

¾ lb pork liver, skinned and
　ducts removed
¾ lb pork, coarsely ground
4oz veal, coarsely ground
8oz pork fat, coarsely ground
1 clove garlic, crushed
2 shallots, finely chopped
8oz bacon strips, rind and
　bones removed

3 tbsps cognac
½ tsp ground allspice
Salt and freshly ground black pepper
1 tsp chopped fresh thyme or sage
4oz smoked tongue or ham, cut into
　¼ inch cubes
2 tbsps heavy cream
1 large bay leaf

Preheat the oven to 350°F. Place the liver in a food processor and process once or twice to chop roughly. Add the ground meats and fat, shallots, garlic, Cognac, allspice, salt and pepper and thyme and process once or twice to mix. Do not over-work the mixture; it should be coarse. Stretch the strips of bacon with the back of a knife and line a terrine, metal baking pan or ovenproof glass dish. Stir the cream and the cubed tongue or ham into the meat mixture by hand and press it into the dish on top of the bacon.

Place the bay leaf on top and fold over any overlapping edges of bacon. Cover the dish with a tight-fitting lid or two layers of foil and place the dish in a bain marie (dish of hand hot water) to come halfway up the sides of the terrine. Bake the pâté for 2 hours, or until the juices are clear. When it is done, remove it from the oven and remove the foil or lid.

Cover with fresh foil and weight down the pâté with cans of food or balance scale weights. Allow to cool at room temperature and then refrigerate the pâté, still weighted, until completely chilled and firm. To serve, remove the weights and foil. Turn the pâté out and scrape off the fat. Slice through the bacon into thin slices.

Potage à l'Oignon Gratiné

Preparation Time: 20 minutes **Cooking Time:** 50-60 minutes **Serves:** 4-6

Originally a Parisian specialty, every region in France now has a recipe for onion soup.

Ingredients

2oz butter or margarine
2lbs onions, peeled and thinly sliced
2 tsps sugar
Pinch salt and pepper

1½ tbsps flour
1 tsp dried thyme
7 cups brown stock
½ cup dry white wine

Crôutes

12 x 1 inch slices French bread
1 tbsp olive oil

8oz grated Gruyère cheese

Melt the butter in a large saucepan over a moderate heat. Stir in the onions and add the sugar. Cook, uncovered, over low heat, stirring occasionally, for 20-30 minutes or until the onions are golden brown. Sprinkle the flour over the onions and cook for 2-3 minutes. Pour on the stock and stir to blend the flour. Add salt, pepper and thyme and return the soup to low heat. Simmer, partially covered, for another 30-40 minutes. Allow the soup to stand while preparing the crôutes.

Brush each side of the slices of bread lightly with olive oil and place them on a baking sheet. Bake in a preheated oven, 325°F, for about 15 minutes. Turn the slices over and bake for a further 15 minutes, or until the bread is dry and lightly browned.

To serve, skim fat from the soup and ladle soup into a tureen or individual soup bowls. Place the crôutes on top of the soup and sprinkle over the grated cheese. Place the soup in a hot oven and bake for 10-20 minutes, or until the cheese has melted. Brown under a preheated broiler, if desired, before serving.

Salade Niçoise

Preparation Time: 20 minutes **Cooking Time:** 9-10 minutes **Serves:** 4-6

Almost everyone knows what Salade Niçoise is, but there are so many variations that it need never be ordinary.

Ingredients

1 head Romaine lettuce
2 hard-cooked eggs, quartered
2 large tomatoes, quartered
6 anchovy fillets
10 pitted black olives

1 tbsp capers
¼ cucumber, diced but not peeled
1 can tuna fish, drained
4 large artichoke hearts, quartered

Dressing

⅓ cup olive oil
2 tbsps white or red wine vinegar
½ clove garlic, crushed

1 tsp mustard
Salt, pepper and lemon juice

Wash the lettuce well, pat dry and break into bite-size pieces. Prepare the remaining ingredients and toss with the lettuce in a large bowl, taking care not to break up the eggs. Mix the dressing ingredients together and whisk until well emulsified. Pour the dressing over the salad just before serving.

The French Alps offer a challenge to skiers of all abilities.

Gougère au Jambon

Preparation Time: 30 minutes **Cooking Time:** 30-45 minutes **Serves:**4-6

This savory pastry dish originated in Burgundy, but is also popular in the Champagne district and indeed in many other districts as well. Serve it as an appetizer or main course.

Ingredients
Choux Pastry
½ cup water
4 tbsps butter or margarine
2oz all-purpose flour, sifted
2 eggs, beaten
½ cup cheese, finely diced
Pinch salt, pepper and dry mustard
Ham Salpicon
1 tbsp butter or margarine

1 tbsp flour
½ cup stock
2oz mushrooms, sliced
2 tsps chopped fresh herbs
Salt and pepper
4oz cooked ham, cut into
  julienne strips
2 tbsps grated cheese and dry
  breadcrumbs mixed

Preheat oven to 400°F. Place the water for the pastry in a small saucepan. Cut the butter into small pieces and add to the water. Bring slowly to boil, making sure that the butter is completely melted before the water comes to a rapid boil. Turn up the heat and allow to boil rapidly for 30 seconds. Sift the flour with a pinch of salt onto a sheet of paper. Take the pan off the heat and tip all the flour in at once. Stir quickly and vigorously until the mixture comes away from the sides of the pan. Spread onto a plate to cool.

Melt the butter in a small saucepan for the salpicon and add the flour. Cook for 1-2 minutes until pale straw colored. Gradually whisk in the stock until smooth. Add a pinch of salt and pepper and the chopped herbs. Stir in the sliced mushrooms and ham and set aside.

To continue with the pastry, add salt, pepper and dry mustard to the paste and return it to the saucepan. Gradually add the egg to the paste mixture, beating well between each addition – this may done by hand, with an electric mixer or in a food processor. It may not be necessary to add all the egg. The mixture should be smooth and shiny and hold its shape when ready. If it is still too thick, beat in the remaining egg. Stir in the diced cheese by hand. Spoon the mixture into a large ovenproof dish, pushing the mixture slightly up the sides of the dish and leaving a well in the center. Fill the center with the ham salpicon and scatter over 2 tbsps grated cheese and dry breadcrumbs, mixed. Bake until the pastry is puffed and browned. Serve immediately.

Omelette Roussillon

Preparation Time: 15 minutes **Cooking Time:** 4-5 minutes **Makes:** 1 omelet

Roussillon is on France's border with Spain. The Spanish influence is evident in the use of tomatoes and peppers combined with eggs.

Ingredients

3 eggs
Salt and pepper
1 tbsp butter or margarine
¼ green pepper, cut into small dice

2 tomatoes, peeled, seeded and
  roughly chopped
2oz ham, cut into small dice

Break the eggs into a bowl, season with salt and pepper and beat to mix thoroughly. Heat an omelet pan and drop in the butter, swirling it so that it coats the bottom and sides. When the butter stops foaming, add pepper and ham. Cook for 1-2 minutes to soften slightly, and add the tomatoes. Pour in the eggs and, as they begin to cook, push the cooked portion with the flat of the fork to allow the uncooked portion underneath. Continue to lift the eggs and shake the pan to prevent them from sticking. When the egg on top is still slightly creamy, fold ⅓ of the omelet to the center and tip it out of the pan onto a warm serving dish, folded side down. Serve immediately.

The Arc du Carrousel stands in the graceful Tuileries Gardens in Paris.

Quiche Lorraine

Preparation Time: 25 minutes **Cooking Time:** 40 minutes **Serves:** 6

The history of this egg and bacon flan goes back to the 16th century in the Lorraine region. Traditionally it doesn't contain cheese, but it's a tasty addition.

Ingredients
Pâte Brisée
4oz butter
6oz all-purpose flour, sifted

Pinch salt
1 egg
2 tsps ice water

Filling
6 strips bacon, cut into large dice
1 tsp butter or margarine
2 shallots, finely chopped
2 eggs plus 2 egg yolks

1 cup heavy cream
Salt, pepper and grated nutmeg
¾cup grated Gruyère cheese
  (optional)

Preheat the oven to 375°F. To prepare the pastry, sift the flour and salt into a large bowl. Rub in the butter until the mixture looks like fine breadcrumbs – this may also be done in a food processor. Beat the egg lightly and mix into the flour by hand or with the machine. If the dough seems crumbly, add some of the water. Chill well before using. Roll the pastry out to a circle about ¼-inch thick on a well-floured surface. Roll the pastry over a rolling pin and unroll it onto a 8-9 inch flan dish. Gently press the pastry into the bottom and up the sides of the dish, being careful not to stretch it. Trim off the excess pastry by running the rolling pin over the rim of the dish or using a sharp knife. Prick the bottom of the pastry lightly with a fork. Place a circle of wax paper on top of the pastry and fill with dry beans, or rice. Bake for about 10 minutes, remove the paper and filling. Prick base again lightly and return to the oven for another 3 minutes or until just beginning to brown. Allow the pastry to cool while preparing the filling.

Place the bacon in a small frying pan and fry over gentle heat until the fat begins to run. Raise the heat and cook until lightly browned and crisp. Place the bacon on paper towels to drain and add the butter to the pan if insufficient fat left. Add the chopped shallots and cook until just beginning to color. Remove to the paper towel to drain with the bacon. Beat the eggs and extra yolks, cream and seasonings together in a large bowl. Scatter the bacon and shallots over the bottom of the pastry case and ladle the custard filling on top of it. If using cheese, add with the custard. Bake in the top half of the oven for about 25 minutes, or until the custard has puffed and browned and a knife inserted into the center comes out clean. Allow to cool slightly and then remove from the dish, or serve directly from the dish.

Truite Meunière aux Herbes

Preparation Time: 15-20 minutes **Cooking Time:** 5-8 minutes **Serves:** 4

The miller (meunier) caught trout fresh from the mill stream and his wife used the flour which was on hand to dredge them with, or so the story goes.

Ingredients

4 even-sized trout, cleaned
   and trimmed
Flour
Salt and pepper
½ cup butter

Juice of 1 lemon
2 tbsps chopped fresh herbs such
   as parsley, chervil, tarragon,
   thyme or marjoram
Lemon wedges to garnish

Trim the trout tails to make them more pointed. Rinse the trout well. Dredge the trout with flour and shake off the excess. Season with salt and pepper. Heat half the butter in a very large sauté pan and, when foaming, place in the trout. It may be necessary to cook the trout in two batches to avoid overcrowding the pan. Cook over fairly high heat on both sides to brown evenly. Depending on size, the trout should take 5-8 minutes per side to cook. The dorsal fin will pull out easily when the trout are cooked. Remove the trout to a serving dish and keep them warm.

Wipe out the pan and add the remaining butter. Cook over moderate heat until beginning to brown, then add the lemon juice and herbs. When the lemon juice is added, the butter will bubble up and sizzle. Pour immediately over the fish and serve with lemon wedges.

The chic resort of Avoriaz can only be reached by cablecar and its car-free environment is the perfect retreat from the pressures of the outside world.

Rougets à la Provençale

Preparation Time: 30 minutes **Cooking Time:** 40 minutes **Serves:** 4

Red Mullet is a very attractive fish, with a flavor quite like shrimp. It is also known as "woodcock of the sea" because it is often served with the liver left inside.

Ingredients

2 tbsps olive oil
1 clove garlic, crushed
2 shallots, finely chopped
1lb ripe tomatoes, peeled, seeded and sliced
2 tsps chopped marjoram and parsley mixed

⅓ cup dry white wine
Salt, pepper and pinch saffron
Oil for frying
2 small bulbs fennel, quartered and cored
4 red mullet, about 6oz each
Flour mixed with salt and pepper

Heat 2 tbsps olive oil in a deep saucepan and add the garlic and shallots. Cook 1-2 minutes to soften slightly, then add tomatoes, herbs, wine, salt, pepper and saffron. Allow to simmer, uncovered, for 30 minutes and set aside while preparing the fennel and fish. Pour about 4 tbsps oil into a large frying pan or sauté pan. Place over moderate heat and add the fennel. Cook quickly until the fennel is slightly browned. Lower the heat and cook a further 5-10 minutes to soften the fennel.

Scale the fish, remove the gills and clean, leaving in the liver if desired. Wash the fish and dry thoroughly. Trim the fins and roll the fish in seasoned flour, shaking off the excess. When the fennel is tender, remove it from the pan and set it aside. Fry the fish until golden brown on both sides, about 2-3 minutes per side. Arrange the fish in a warm serving dish and surround with the fennel. Reheat the sauce and spoon over the fish. Serve remaining sauce separately.

The marshes and lagoons of the Camargue are home to herds of wild horses.

Raie au Beurre Noir

Preparation Time: 20 minutes **Cooking Time:** 15-20 minutes **Serves:** 4

It is amazing how the addition of simple ingredients like browned butter, vinegar, capers and parsley can turn an ordinary fish into a French masterpiece.

Ingredients

4 wings of skate
1 slice onion
2 parsley stalks

Pinch salt
6 black peppercorns

Beurre Noir

4 tbsps butter
2 tbsps white wine vinegar

1 tbsp capers
1 tbsp chopped parsley (optional)

Place the skate in one layer in a large, deep pan. Completely cover with water and add the onion, parsley stalks, salt and peppercorns. Bring gently to the boil with pan uncovered. Allow to simmer 15-20 minutes, or until the skate is done. Lift the fish out onto a serving dish and remove the skin and any large pieces of bone. Take care not to break up the fish. Place the butter in a small pan and cook over high heat until it begins to brown. Add the capers and immediately remove the butter from the heat. Add the vinegar, which will cause the butter to bubble. Add parsley, if using, and pour immediately over the fish to serve.

Normandy is famous for its large apple crop, which goes to make delicious cider and Calvados – a fiery brandy.

Poulet Fricassée

Preparation Time: 30 minutes **Cooking Time:** 30-40 minutes **Serves:** 4

This is a white stew, enriched and thickened with an egg and cream mixture which is called a liaison in French cooking.

Ingredients

3lb chicken, quartered and skinned
¼ cup butter or margarine
1oz flour
2 cups chicken stock
1 bouquet garni
12-16 small onions, peeled
12oz button mushrooms, whole
   if small, quartered if large

Juice and grated rind of ½ lemon
2 egg yolks
6 tbsps heavy cream
2 tbsps chopped parsley and thyme
Salt and pepper
3 tbsps milk (optional)
Garnish with lemon slices

Melt 3 tbsps of the butter in a large sauté pan or frying pan. Place in the chicken in 1 layer and cook over gentle heat for about 5 minutes, or until the chicken is no longer pink. Do not allow the chicken to brown. If necessary, cook the chicken in two batches. When the chicken is sufficiently cooked, remove it from the pan and set aside. Stir the flour into the butter remaining in the pan and cook over very low heat, stirring continuously for about 1 minute, or until a pale straw color. Remove the pan from the heat and gradually beat in the chicken stock. When blended smoothly, add lemon juice and rind, return the pan to the heat and bring to the boil, whisking constantly. Reduce the heat and allow the sauce to simmer for 1 minute. Return the chicken to the pan with any juices that have accumulated and add the bouquet garni. The sauce should almost cover the chicken. If it does not, add more stock or water. Bring to the boil, cover the pan and reduce the heat. Allow the chicken to simmer gently for 30 minutes.

Meanwhile, melt the remaining butter in a small frying pan, add the onions, cover and cook very gently for 10 minutes. Do not allow the onions to brown. Remove the onions from the pan with a draining spoon and add to the chicken. Cook the mushrooms in the remaining butter for 2 minutes. Set the mushrooms aside and add them to the chicken 10 minutes before the end of cooking. Test the chicken by piercing a thigh portion with a sharp knife. If the juices run clear, the chicken is cooked. Transfer chicken and vegetables to a serving plate and discard the bouquet garni. Skim the sauce of any fat and boil it rapidly to reduce by almost half.

Blend the egg yolks and cream together and whisk-in several spoonfuls of the hot sauce. Return the egg yolk and cream mixture to the remaining sauce and cook gently for 2-3 minutes. Stir the sauce constantly and do not allow it to boil. If very thick, add milk. Adjust the seasoning, stir in the parsley and spoon over the chicken in a serving dish. Garnish with lemon slices.

Coq au Vin

Preparation Time: 30-40 minutes **Cooking Time:** 50 minutes **Serves:** 4

This dish is probably the most famous chicken recipe in all of France.

Ingredients

8oz thick cut bacon strips
1½ cups water
1oz butter or margarine
12-16 button onions or shallots
8oz mushrooms, left whole if
    small, quartered if large
1½ cups dry red wine
3lb chicken, cut into eight pieces
3 tbsps brandy

1 bouquet garni
1 clove garlic, crushed
3 tbsps flour
1½ cups chicken stock
2 tbsps chopped parsley
4 slices bread, crusts removed
Oil for frying
Salt and pepper

Preheat oven to 350°F. Cut the bacon into strips about ¼-inch thick. Bring water to the boil and blanch the bacon by simmering for 5 minutes. Remove the bacon with a draining spoon and dry on paper towels. Re-boil the water and drop in the onions. Allow them to boil rapidly for 2-3 minutes and then plunge into cold water and peel. Set the onions aside with the bacon.

Melt half the butter in a large frying pan and add the bacon and onions. Fry over high heat, stirring frequently and shaking the pan, until the bacon and onions are golden brown. Remove them with a draining spoon and leave on paper towels. Add the remaining butter to the saucepan and cook the mushrooms for 1-2 minutes. Remove them and set them aside with the onions and bacon.

Reheat the frying pan and brown the chicken, a few pieces at a time. When it is all browned, transfer it to a large ovenproof casserole. Pour the wine into a small saucepan and boil it to reduce to about 1 cup. Pour the brandy into a small saucepan or ladle and warm over low heat. Ignite with a match and pour the brandy (while still flaming) over the chicken. Shake the casserole carefully until the flames die down. If the brandy should flare up, cover quickly with the casserole lid. Add the bouquet garni and garlic to the casserole.

Pour off all but 1 tbsp of fat from the frying pan and stir in the flour. Cook over gentle heat, scraping any of the browned chicken juices from the bottom of the pan. Pour in the reduced wine and add the stock. Bring the sauce to the boil over high heat, stirring constantly until thickened. Strain over the chicken in the casserole and cover tightly. Place in the oven and cook for 20 minutes. After that time, add the bacon, onions and mushrooms and continue cooking for a further 15-20 minutes, or until the chicken is tender. Remove the bouquet garni and season with salt and pepper. Cut each of the bread slices into 4 triangles. Heat enough oil in a large frying pan to cover the triangles of bread. When the oil is very hot, add the bread triangles two at a time and fry until golden brown and crisp. Drain on paper towels. To serve, arrange the chicken in a deep dish, pour over the sauce and vegetables and arrange the fried bread croûtes around the outside of the dish. Sprinkle with chopped parsley.

Poulet Sauté Vallée d'Auge

Preparation Time: 25-30 minutes **Cooking Time:** 55-60 minutes **Serves:** 4

This dish contains all the ingredients that Normandy is famous for – butter, cream, apples and Calvados.

Ingredients

2oz butter or margarine
2 tbsps oil
3lbs chicken, cut into eight pieces
4 tbsps Calvados
1/3 cup chicken stock
2 apples, peeled, cored and
    coarsely chopped

2 sticks celery, finely chopped
1 shallot, finely chopped
1/2 tsp dried thyme, crumbled
1/3 cup heavy cream
2 egg yolks, lightly beaten
Salt and white pepper

Garnish

1 bunch watercress or small
    parsley sprigs
2 apples, quartered, cored and
    cut into cubes

2 tbsps butter
Sugar

Melt half the butter and all of the oil in a large sauté pan over moderate heat. When the foam begins to subside, brown the chicken, a few pieces at a time, skin side down first. When all the chicken is browned, pour off most of the fat from the pan and return the chicken to the pan. Pour the Calvados into a ladle or small saucepan and warm over gentle heat. Ignite with a match and pour, while still flaming, over the chicken. Shake the sauté pan gently until the flames subside. If the Calvados should flare up, cover the pan immediately with the lid. Pour over the stock and scrape any browned chicken juices from the bottom of the pan. Set the chicken aside. Melt the remaining butter in a small saucepan or frying pan. Cook the chopped apples, shallot and celery and the thyme for about 10 minutes or until soft but not brown. Spoon over the chicken and return the pan to the high heat. Bring to the boil, then reduce heat, cover the pan and simmer 50 minutes. When the chicken is cooked, beat the eggs and cream. With a whisk, gradually beat in some of the hot sauce. Pour the mixture back into a saucepan and cook over low heat for 2-3 minutes, stirring constantly until the sauce thickens and coats the back of a spoon. Season the sauce with salt and white pepper and set it aside while preparing the garnish.

Put the butter in a small frying pan and when foaming, add the apple. Toss over a high heat until beginning to soften. Sprinkle with sugar and cook until the apple begins to caramelize. To serve, coat the chicken with the sauce and decorate with watercress or parsley. Spoon the caramelized apples over the chicken.

Poulet Grillé au Limon

Preparation Time: 25 minutes & 4 hours marinating **Cooking Time:** 35 minutes
Serves: 4

Crisp chicken with a tang of limes makes an elegant yet quickly-made entreé.
From the warm regions of southern France, it is perfect for a summer meal.

Ingredients

2lb chicken
4 limes
1 tsp basil

6 tbsps olive oil
Salt, pepper and sugar

Remove the leg ends, neck and wing tips from the chicken and discard them.
Split the chicken in half, cutting away the backbone completely and discarding
it. Loosen the ball and socket joint in the leg and flatten each half of the
chicken by hitting it with the flat side of a cleaver. Season the chicken on both
sides with salt and pepper and sprinkle over the basil. Place the chicken in a
shallow dish and pour over 2 tbsps of olive oil. Squeeze the juice from 2 of the
limes over the chicken. Cover and leave to marinate in the refrigerator for 4
hours.

    Heat the broiler to its highest setting and preheat the oven to 375°F.
Remove the chicken from the marinade and place in the broiler pan. Cook one
side until golden brown and turn the pieces over. Sprinkle with 1 tbsps olive oil
and brown the other side. Place the chicken in a roasting dish, sprinkle with
the remaining oil and roast in the oven for about 25 minutes. Peel the
remaining limes and slice them thinly. When the chicken is cooked, place the
lime slices on top and sprinkle lightly with sugar. Place under the broiler for a
few minutes to caramelize the sugar and cook the limes. Place in a serving
dish and spoon over any remaining marinade and the cooking juices. Serve
immediately.

With its casino, nightclubs and yacht harbor, the town of Cabourg in Normandy is a
popular stopping point for tourists.

Rognons à la Dijonnaise

Preparation Time: 25 minutes **Cooking Time:** 15-17 minutes **Serves:** 6

Veal kidneys are lighter in color and milder in flavor than lamb's kidneys. Since they must be quickly cooked, kidneys make an ideal sauté dish.

Ingredients

½ cup unsalted butter
3-4 whole veal kidneys
1-2 shallots, finely chopped
1 cup dry white wine

⅓ cup butter, softened
3 tbsps Dijon mustard
Salt, pepper and lemon juice to taste
2 tbsps chopped parsley

Melt the unsalted butter in a large sauté pan. Cut the kidneys into 1-inch pieces and remove any fat or core. When the butter stops foaming, add the kidneys and sauté them, uncovered, until they are light brown on all sides – about 10 minutes. Remove the kidneys from the pan and keep them warm. Add the shallots to the pan and cook for about 1 minute, stirring frequently. Add the wine and bring to the boil, stirring constantly and scraping the pan to remove any browned juices. Allow to boil rapidly for 3-4 minutes until the wine is reduced to about 3 tbsps. Remove the pan from the heat. Mix the remaining butter with the mustard, add salt and pepper and whisk the mixture into the reduced sauce. Return the kidneys to the pan, add the lemon juice and parsley and cook over low heat for 1-2 minutes to heat through. Serve immediately.

Entrevaux was once a fortress town and much of its medieval heritage remains.

Carbonnade à la Flamande

Preparation Time: 30 minutes **Cooking Time:** 2-2¾ hours **Serves:** 6

This carbonnade is a rich stew cooked in the Flemish style with dark beer.

Ingredients

2 tbsps oil
1½lbs braising steak
1 large onion, thinly sliced
2 tbsps flour
1 clove garlic, crushed
1 cup brown ale
1 cup hot water

Bouquet garni, salt and pepper
Pinch sugar and nutmeg
Dash red wine vinegar
6 slices French bread cut about
    ½-inch thick
French or Dijon mustard

Preheat the oven to 325°F. Place the oil in a large, heavy-based frying pan. Cut the meat into 2-inch pieces and brown quickly on both sides in the oil. Brown the meat 5-6 pieces at a time to avoid crowding the pan. Remove the meat when browned, lower the heat and add the onion. Cook until the onion is beginning to soften and color. Stir in the flour and add the garlic. Add the hot water and ale. Add the bouquet garni, season with salt and pepper, add the sugar, nutmeg and vinegar. Bring to the boil on top of the stove. Transfer to an ovenproof casserole with the meat, cover and cook in the oven for 2-2½ hours.

Fifteen minutes before serving, skim off any fat from the surface and reserve it. Spread the mustard on the bread and spoon some of the fat over each slice. Place the bread on top of the casserole, pushing it down slightly. Cook a further 15-20 minutes, uncovered, or until the bread is browned and crisp.

The picturesque chateaux of France attract visitors to many peaceful rural areas.

Filet de Porc aux Pruneaux

Preparation Time: 25 minutes **Cooking Time:** 45 minutes **Serves:** 4-6

Tours, situated on the River Loire, is where this dish originated. It is a rich dish with its creamy sauce and wine-soaked prunes.

Ingredients

2-3 small pork fillets	1-2 tbsps flour
1lb pitted prunes	Salt and pepper
2 cups white wine	1 tbsp redcurrant jelly
3 tbsps butter or margarine	1 cup heavy cream

Soak the prunes in the white wine for about 1 hour and then put them into a very low oven to soften further. If the prunes are the ready-softened variety, soak for 20 minutes and omit the oven cooking. Slice the pork fillet on the diagonal into 1-inch-thick pieces. Flatten them slightly with the palm of the hand. Dredge them with the flour, and melt the butter in a heavy pan. When the butter is foaming, put in the pork and cook until lightly browned on both sides. It may be necessary to cook the pork fillet in several batches. Add half the soaking liquid from the prunes, cover the pan and cook very gently on moderate heat for about 45 minutes. If necessary, add more wine from the prunes while the pork is cooking.

When the pork is tender, pour liquid into a small saucepan and bring to the boil. Reduce by about ¼ and add the redcurrant jelly. Stir until dissolved and then add the cream. Bring the sauce back to the boil and allow to boil rapidly, stirring frequently. When the sauce is reduced and thickened slightly, pour over the meat and reheat. Add the prunes and transfer to a serving dish. Sprinkle with chopped parsley if desired.

Val d'Isere, France's most famous ski resort, looks very different in summer.

Ragoût de Veau Marengo

Preparation Time: 30 minutes **Cooking Time:** 1-1½ hours **Serves:** 6

There is an Italian influence evident in this stew recipe. Pie veal is relatively inexpensive, thus making this recipe easier on the budget than most veal dishes.

Ingredients

3lbs lean pie veal
4 tbsps flour, mixed with salt
 and pepper
4 tbsps olive oil
2 shallots, finely chopped
½ clove garlic, crushed
⅓ cup dry white wine
1 cup brown stock

8oz canned tomatoes, drained
 and crushed
1 bouquet garni
2 strips lemon peel
4oz mushrooms, whole if small,
 quartered if large
3 tbsps butter or margarine
2 tbsps chopped parsley (optional)

Preheat oven to 325°F. Dredge the pieces of veal with the seasoned flour. Pour the oil into a large sauté pan or heatproof casserole and place over a moderate heat. When the oil is hot, cook the veal 5-10 pieces at a time, depending upon the size of the pan. Brown the veal well on all sides, remove from the pan and set aside. Add the shallots and garlic to the pan, lower the heat and cook until softened, but not colored. Return the veal to the pan, add the wine, stock, tomatoes, bouquet garni and lemon peel. Bring to the boil on top of the stove, cover and cook in the oven for 1¼ hours, or until the veal is tender.

Meanwhile, melt the remaining butter in a frying pan and add the mushrooms and toss over a moderate heat for 2-3 minutes, stirring occasionally. When the veal is cooked, skim the surface of the sauce to remove excess fat and add the mushrooms with their cooking liquid to the veal. Cook for a further 10-15 minutes then remove the bouquet garni and the lemon peel. Transfer the veal and mushrooms to a serving dish and reduce the sauce to about 1½ cups by boiling rapidly. Adjust the seasoning and pour the sauce over the veal and mushrooms before serving. Reheat if necessary and garnish with chopped parsley, if desired.

Navarin Printanier

Preparation Time: 30-40 minutes **Cooking Time:** 30-35 minutes **Serves:** 6

This is a ragôut or brown stew traditionally made with mutton chops. Substitute lamb for a milder taste. Printanier means that a selection of vegetables is added.

Ingredients

¹/₃ cup vegetable oil
12 even-sized lamb cutlets
Flour mixed with salt, pepper and
    a pinch dried thyme
2 shallots, finely chopped
1 clove garlic, crushed

2 cups brown stock
½ cup dry white wine
5 tomatoes, peeled, seeded
    and coarsely chopped
1 bouquet garni

Spring Vegetables

12 new potatoes, scrubbed
    but not peeled
8 baby carrots, scraped (if green tops
    are in good condition, leave on)
6 small turnips, peeled and left whole
12oz frozen petits pois

8oz green beans cut into 1 inch
    lengths on the diagonal
12 green onions, roots ends trimmed
    and green tops trimmed about
    3 inches from the ends
1 tbsps chopped parsley (optional)

Preheat the oven to 350°F. Heat about half the oil in a large, heavy-based frying pan. Dredge the lamb cutlets with the flour mixture, shaking off the excess. Brown the lamb cutlets 4 at a time, adding more oil if necessary. When the cutlets are brown on all sides, remove them to a heavy casserole. Remove most of the oil from the pan and cook the shallots and garlic over moderate heat, stirring constantly. Add the stock and bring to the boil, scraping the bottom of the pan to remove the browned meat juices. Allow to boil rapidly to reduce slightly, then add the tomatoes. Pour the sauce over the lamb, turning the cutlets to coat all of them with the sauce. Add the bouquet garni, cover tightly and cook in the oven for about 30 minutes, or until the lamb is tender. After about 10 minutes, add the potatoes and carrots to the lamb. Add the turnips, green beans, peas and green onions 15 minutes before the end of cooking time.

    After 30 minutes, remove the lamb and any vegetables that are tender. Boil the sauce rapidly to reduce it and cook any vegetables that need extra time. Pour the sauce over the lamb and vegetables to serve and sprinkle with chopped parsley, if desired.

Pommes Dauphiné

Preparation Time: 25 minutes **Cooking Time:** 30-40 minutes **Serves:** 6

The food from the mountainous province of Dauphiné is robust fare. Comté is the finest cheese of the area and like Gruyère it is creamy rather than stringy when melted.

Ingredients

1 clove garlic, peeled and crushed
   with the flat of a knife
1oz butter
2¼lbs potatoes, peeled and
   thinly sliced

½ cup light cream
Salt and pepper
6oz grated Comté or Gruyère cheese
3oz butter cut into very small dice

Preheat the oven to 400°F. Rub the bottom and sides of a heavy baking dish with the crushed clove of garlic. Grease the bottom and sides liberally with the butter. Use a dish that can also be employed as a serving dish. Spread half of the potato slices in the bottom of the dish, sprinkle with cheese, salt and pepper and dot with the butter dice. Top with the remaining slices of potato, neatly arranged. Sprinkle with the remaining cheese, salt, pepper and butter. Pour the cream into the side of the dish around the potatoes. Cook in the top part of the oven for 30-40 minutes, or until the potatoes are tender and the top is nicely browned. Serve immediately.

Carcassonne, in the Languedoc region, is Europe's largest medieval fortress, with towers dating back to the 5th century.

Haricots Verts à l'Oignon

Preparation Time: 15 minutes **Cooking Time:** 8-10 minutes **Serves:** 4-6

These slender green beans are the classic French vegetable. Quickly blanched, then refreshed under cold water, they can be reheated and still stay beautifully green.

Ingredients
1lb French beans
1oz butter

1 medium onion
Salt and pepper

Top and tail the beans. Cook the beans whole in boiling salted water for about 8-10 minutes. Meanwhile, finely chop the onion. Melt the butter and fry the finely chopped onion until lightly brown. Drain the beans and toss them over heat to dry. Pour the butter and onions over the beans and season with salt and pepper. Serve immediately.

The Arc de Triomphe by night from the Champs Elysees.

Tomates à la Languedocienne

Preparation Time: 15 minutes **Cooking Time:** 5-8 minutes **Serves:** 4

This dish from the Languedoc region of southern France is similar to Provençal tomatoes, but is not as strong in flavor.

Ingredients

4 large ripe tomatoes
2 slices white bread, crusts removed
1 clove garlic, crushed
2 tbsps olive oil

1 tbsp chopped parsley
2 tsp chopped thyme or marjoram
Salt and pepper

Cut the tomatoes in half and score the cut surface. Sprinkle with salt and leave upside-down in a colander to drain. Allow the tomatoes to drain for 1-2 hours. Rinse the tomatoes and scoop out most of the juice and pulp.

Mix the olive oil and garlic together and brush both sides of the bread with the mixture, leaving it to soften. Chop the herbs and the bread together until well mixed. Press the filling into the tomatoes and sprinkle with any remaining garlic and olive oil mixture.

Cook the tomatoes in a ovenproof dish under a preheated broiler under low heat for the first 5 minutes. Then raise the dish or the heat to brown the tomatoes on top. Serve immediately.

Near the ancient port of Marseille is the small, picturesque fishing port of Cassis.

Fèves au Jambon

Preparation Time: 20-30 minutes **Cooking Time:** 15 minutes **Serves:** 6

Touraine, where this dish comes from, is often called the "Garden of France." Some of the finest vegetables in the country are grown there.

Ingredients
2lbs broad beans
½ cup heavy cream

2oz ham, cut into thin strips
1 tbsp chopped parsley or chervil

If using fresh beans, remove them from their pods. Cook the beans in boiling salted water until tender, drain and keep warm. Combine the cream and ham in a small saucepan. Add a pinch of salt and pepper and bring to the boil. Boil rapidly for 5 minutes to thicken the cream. If desired, peel the outer skins from the beans before tossing with the cream and ham. Add parsley or chervil, adjust the seasoning and reheat if necessary. Serve immediately.

The Eiffel Tower is still one of Paris' most popular tourist attractions although it was considered hideous when it was completed in 1889.

Ratatouille

Cooking Time: 35 minutes   **Serves:** 6-8

This is probably one of the most familiar dishes from southern France. Either hot or cold, it's full of the warm sun of Provence.

Ingredients

2 eggplants, sliced and scored
　　on both sides
4-6 zucchini, depending on size
3-6 tbsps olive oil
2 onions, peeled and thinly sliced
2 green peppers, seeded and cut
　　into 1 inch pieces

2 tsps chopped fresh basil or
　　1 tsp dried basil
1 large clove garlic, crushed
2lbs ripe tomatoes, peeled
　　and quartered
Salt and pepper
½ cup dry white wine

Lightly salt the eggplant slices and place on paper towels to drain for about 30 minutes. Rinse and pat dry. Slice the zucchini thickly and set them aside. Pour 3 tbsps of the olive oil into a large frying pan and when hot, lightly brown the onions, green peppers and zucchini slices. Remove the vegetables to a casserole and add the eggplant slices to the frying pan or saucepan. Cook to brown both sides lightly and place in the casserole with the other vegetables. Add extra oil while frying the vegetables as needed. Add the garlic and tomatoes to the oil and cook for 1 minute. Add the garlic and tomatoes to the rest of the vegetables along with any remaining olive in the frying pan. Add basil, salt, pepper and wine and bring to the boil over moderate heat. Cover and reduce to simmering. If the vegetables need moisture during cooking, add a little white wine. When the vegetables are tender, remove them from the casserole to a serving dish and boil any remaining liquid in the pan rapidly to reduce to about 2 tbsps. Pour over the ratatouille to serve.

The Tour de France is the world's most prestigious cycle event.

Crêpes au Chocolat et Framboises

Preparation Time: 30 minutes **Cooking Time:** 30 minutes **Serves:** 6

Crêpes Suzette may be more famous, but these, filled with chocolate and raspberry, are incredibly delicious.

Ingredients
Crêpe Batter
1½ cups milk and water mixed
4 eggs
Pinch salt

2 cups all-purpose flour, sifted
1 tbsp sugar
4 tbsps melted butter or oil

Filling
8oz semi-sweet dessert chocolate, grated
4oz seedless raspberry jam

Whipped cream and chopped, browned hazelnuts

Put all the ingredients for the crêpe batter into a food processor or blender and process for about 1 minute, pushing down the sides occasionally. Process a few seconds more to blend thoroughly. Leave, covered, in a cool place for 30 minutes to 1 hour. The consistency of the batter should be that of thin cream. Add more milk if necessary. Brush a crêpe pan or small frying pan lightly with oil and place over high heat. When a slight haze forms, pour a large spoonful of the batter into the pan and swirl the pan to cover the base. Pour out any excess into a separate bowl. Cook on one side until just beginning to brown around the edges. Turn over and cook on the other side until lightly speckled with brown. Slide each crêpe onto a plate and repeat using the remaining batter. Reheat the pan occasionally in-between cooking each crêpe. The amount of batter should make 12 crêpes. As the crêpes are cooked, sprinkle them evenly with grated chocolate and divide the raspberry jam among all the crêpes. Roll them up so that the jam shows at the ends, or fold into triangles. Reheat in a moderate oven for about 10 minutes before serving. Top with whipped cream and a sprinkling of browned nuts.

Soufflé au Citron Froid

Preparation Time: 25-30 minutes   **Serves:** 6

A cold soufflé is really a mousse in disguise. It doesn't "rise" in the refrigerator, but is set above the rim of its dish with the help of a paper collar and gelatin.

Ingredients
3 eggs, separated
¾ cup sugar
Grated rind and juice of
　2 small lemons

1 tbsp gelatin dissolved in
　3-4 tbsps water
¾ cup cream, lightly whipped

Decoration
½ cup cream, whipped
Thin strips lemon rind or lemon twists

Finely chopped almonds or pistachios

Tie a double thickness of wax paper around a soufflé dish to stand about 3 inches above the rim of the dish. Beat the egg yolks in a large bowl until thick and lemon colored. Add the sugar gradually and then the lemon rind and juice. Set the bowl over a pan of hot water and whisk until the mixture is thick and leaves a ribbon trail. Remove the bowl from the heat and whisk a few minutes longer. Melt the gelatin and the water until clear, pour into the lemon mixture and stir thoroughly. Set the bowl over ice and stir until beginning to thicken. Whip the egg whites until stiff but not dry and fold into the lemon mixture along with the lightly whipped cream. Pour into the prepared soufflé dish and chill in the refrigerator until the gelatin sets completely. To serve, peel off the paper carefully and spread some of the cream on the sides of the mixture. Press finely chopped nuts into the cream. Pipe the remaining cream into rosettes on top of the soufflé and decorate with strips of rind or lemon twists.

The wild and rugged coast near Quiberon, in Brittany.

Mousse au Chocolat Basque

Preparation Time: 20 minutes **Cooking Time:** 10 minutes **Serves:** 6

This mousse is a dark chocolate mixture which sets to a rich cream in the refrigerator. Chilling overnight makes it even better.

Ingredients

6oz semi-sweet chocolate
Scant ⅓ cup water
1 tbsp butter

3 eggs, separated
2 tbsps rum

Chop the chocolate into small pieces and combine with the water in a heavy-based saucepan. Cook over very gentle heat so that the chocolate and water form a thick cream. Remove from the heat, allow to cool slightly and then beat in the butter. Add the rum and beat in the egg yolks one at a time.

Whip the egg whites until stiff but not dry and fold thoroughly into the chocolate mixture. Pour into small pots or ramekins and chill overnight. Finish with whipped cream and chocolate curls to serve, if desired.

The Trocadero Gardens near the Eiffel Tower offer a quiet respite from the tourists and the traffic.

Poires au Vin Rouge

Preparation Time: 25 minutes **Cooking Time:** 20 minutes **Serves:** 6

A marvellous recipe for using firm cooking pears to their best advantage. They look beautiful served in a glass bowl.

Ingredients

2 cups dry red wine
Juice of half lemon
1 strip lemon peel
1 cup sugar

1 small piece stick cinnamon
6 small ripe but firm pears, peeled,
 but with the stalks left on

Bring the wine, lemon juice and peel, sugar and cinnamon to the boil in a deep saucepan or ovenproof casserole that will accommodate 6 pears snugly. Stir until the sugar dissolves and then allow to boil rapidly for 1 minute. Peel the pears lengthwise and remove the small eye from the bottom of each pear. Place the pears upright in the simmering wine. Allow to cook slowly for 20 minutes, or until they are soft but not mushy. If the syrup does not completely cover the pears, allow the pears to cook on their sides and turn and baste them frequently. Cool the pears in the syrup until lukewarm and then remove them. Remove the cinnamon stick and the lemon peel and discard. If the syrup is still very thin, remove pears, boil to reduce slightly or mix 1 tbsp arrowroot with a little cold water, add some of the warm syrup and return the arrowroot to the rest of the syrup. Bring to the boil, stirring constantly until thickened and cleared. Spoon the syrup over the pears and refrigerate or serve warm. Pears may be decorated with flaked toasted almonds and served with lightly whipped cream if desired.

A still summer night brings people onto the streets of Paris to see and be seen.

Eclairs

Preparation Time: 40 minutes **Cooking Time:** 30-40 minutes **Makes:** 12

Think of French pastry and eclairs immediately spring to mind.

Ingredients
Choux Pastry
⅞ cup water
⅓ cup butter or margarine

¾ cup all-purpose flour, sifted
3 eggs

Crème Patissière
1 whole egg
1 egg yolk
¼ cup sugar
1 tbsp cornstarch

1½ tbsps flour
1 cup milk
Few drops vanilla extract

Glacé Icing
1lb confectioners' sugar
Hot water

Few drops vanilla extract

Preheat oven to 350°F. Combine the water and butter for the pastry in a deep saucepan and bring to the boil. Once boiling rapidly, take the pan off the heat. Stir in the flour all at once and beat just until the mixture leaves the sides of the pan. Spread out onto a plate to cool. When cool, return to the saucepan and gradually add the beaten egg. Beat in well in between each addition of egg until the paste is smooth and shiny – should be of soft dropping consistency, but holding its shape well. It may not be necessary to add all the egg. Pipe or spoon into strips of about 3 inches long, spaced well apart on lightly-greased baking sheets. Sprinkle the sheets lightly with water and place in the oven. Immediately increase oven temperature to 375°F. Make sure the pastry is very crisp before removing it from the oven, this will take about 20-30 minutes. If the pastry is not crisp, return to the oven for a further 5 minutes.

To prepare the Crème Patissière, separate the whole egg and reserve the white. Mix the egg yolks and sugar together, sift in the flours and add about half the milk, stirring well. Bring the remainder of the milk to the boil and pour onto the yolk mixture, stirring constantly. Return the mixture to the pan and stir over heat until boiling point is reached. Take off the heat and whip the egg white until stiff but not dry. Fold the egg white into the mixture and return to the heat. Cook gently for about 1 minute, stirring occasionally. Add the vanilla extract at this point. Pour the mixture into a bowl and press a sheet of wax paper directly onto the surface of the crème and leave it to cool.

Sift the confectioners' sugar into a bowl and add hot water, stirring constantly until the mixture is of thick coating consistency. The icing should cover the back of a wooden spoon but run off slowly. Add the vanilla extract.

To assemble the eclairs, cut the choux pastry almost in half lengthways and either pipe or spoon in the Crème Patissière. Coat the top of each eclair with a smooth layer of glacé icing. Allow the icing to set before serving.